W9-ACH-284

Cool
QUICK BREADS

Easy Recipes for Kids to Bake

Pam Price

ABDO
Publishing Company

Visit us at www.abdopublishing.com

Published by ABDO Publishing Company, 8000 West 78th Street, Edina, Minnesota 55439. Copyright © 2010 by Abdo Consulting Group, Inc. International copyrights reserved in all countries. No part of this book may be reproduced in any form without written permission from the publisher. Checkerboard Library™ is a trademark and logo of ABDO Publishing Company.

Printed in the United States of America, North Mankato, Minnesota
092009
012010

 PRINTED ON RECYCLED PAPER

Editor: Liz Salzmann
Series Concept: Nancy Tuminelly
Cover and Interior Design: Anders Hanson, Mighty Media, Inc.
Photo Credits: Anders Hanson, Shutterstock

The following manufacturers/names appearing in this book are trademarks: Arm & Hammer®, Bialetti®, C&H®, KitchenAid, Kraft®, Kraft® Calumet®, Land O' Lakes®, Lunds® and Byerly's®, McCormick®, Morton®, Proctor Silex®, Pyrex®, Roundy's®

Library of Congress Cataloging-in-Publication Data

Price, Pamela S.
  Cool quick breads : easy recipes for kids to bake / Pam Price.
     p. cm. -- (Cool baking)
  Includes index.
  ISBN 978-1-60453-779-6
  1. Bread--Juvenile literature. I. Title.
  TX769.P74 2010
  641.8'15--dc22
                              2009025743

Table of Contents

What Is Quick Bread?

Making quick breads is fast and fun!

Quick breads are quicker to make than yeast breads. That is why they are called quick breads. When you make bread with yeast, you have to let the dough rise. This can take an hour or more. Then you punch down the dough and let it rise again. This process takes hours.

But you make quick breads with baking soda or baking powder instead of yeast. That means you can bake the bread as soon as you mix the batter. Now that's quick!

You may be familiar with quick breads such as banana bread and cornbread. You'll learn how to make both of those in this book. You'll also make some fun breads that use store-bought biscuit dough. So grab your apron and oven mitts. Let's bake!

GET THE PICTURE!

When a step number in a recipe has a colored circle around it, look for the picture that goes with it. The circle around the photo will be the same color as the step number.

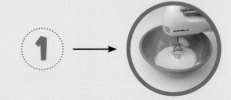

Ready, Set, Bake!

Preparation is a key element of successful baking. Here are some things to keep in mind.

ASK PERMISSION

> Get permission to use the kitchen, baking tools, and ingredients.

> If you'd like to do something by yourself, say so. As long as you can do it safely, do it!

> Ask for help when you need it. Professional chefs have *sous chefs*, which means "assistant chefs" in French. You can have one too!

BE PREPARED

Read the whole recipe the day before you plan to bake.

> Make sure you have all the ingredients. Do you need to go to the grocery store?

> Will there be enough time? For example, cakes need to cool completely before you frost them.

When it's time to bake, these steps will help you be organized.

> Gather all the tools and equipment you will need.

> Prepare the pans as directed and preheat the oven.

> Gather the listed ingredients. Sometimes you need prepared ingredients such as chopped nuts or sifted flour. Do those prep jobs as you gather the ingredients.

> Finally, do the recipe steps in the order they are listed.

Safety First!

When you bake you need to use an oven. Sometimes you also have to use sharp tools. Ask an adult helper to be in the kitchen with you. Here's how to keep it safe.

HOT STUFF

> Set up a cooling rack ahead of time.

> Make sure it's easy to get from the oven to the cooling area. There should be no people or things in the way.

> Always use oven mitts, not towels, when handling hot pots and pans.

> The oven is hot too. Don't bump into the racks or the door.

THAT'S SHARP

> Choose a small knife. Cut just a small amount of food at a time.

> Always keep your other hand away from the blade.

> Work slowly and keep your eyes on the knife.

KEY SYMBOLS

In this book, you will see some symbols beside the recipes. Here is what they mean.

SUPER SHARP!
You need to use a knife for this recipe. Ask an adult to stand by.

SUPER COOL!
This symbol means there are other ways to make the recipe.

Germ Alert!

It's so tempting, but you shouldn't eat batter that contains raw eggs. Raw eggs may contain salmonella **bacteria**, which can cause food poisoning. Eating batter that contains raw eggs might make you sick. Really sick! Ask an adult if it's okay to lick bowls, beaters, and spoons.

KEEP IT CLEAN

> Tie back long hair.

> Wash your hands before you begin baking. Rub them with soap for 20 seconds before rinsing. Wash them again if you eat, sneeze, cough, take a bathroom break, or touch the trash container.

> Use clean tools and equipment. If you lick a spoon, wash it before using it again.

> Make sure that your cutting board hasn't had raw meat on it.

Tools of the Trade

These are the basic tools and equipment used for baking quick breads.
Each recipe in this book lists the tools you will need.

MEASURING CUPS

MEASURING SPOONS

LOAF PAN

8-INCH SQUARE PAN

MIXER AND BEATERS

WHISK

MUFFIN PAN

SILICONE SPATULA

MIXING BOWLS

WOODEN SPOON

TUBE PAN OR BUNDT PAN

GRATER

PLASTIC BAG

SMALL SAUCEPAN

GARLIC PRESS

PASTRY BRUSH

SIFTER

ZESTER

KITCHEN SCISSORS

OVEN MITTS

KNIFE AND CUTTING BOARD

COOLING RACK

9

Cool Ingredients

Butter, flour, sugar. You can make many different goodies based on these three ingredients! Add a few others, and the possibilities are endless.

BUTTER AND OIL

Always choose unsalted butter for baking. You add salt in most recipes. Using unsalted butter keeps the batter from having too much salt.

Some recipes will call for oil instead of butter. Oils are made by crushing and pressing seeds and other parts of plants. In recipes that call for oil, use canola oil if you can.

FLOUR

In a recipe, the word *flour* means all-purpose wheat flour. But other grains can be ground into flour too. Some of these grains include kamut, rye, buckwheat, and corn.

SUGAR

You use several types of sugar for baking. Most common are granulated sugar, powdered sugar, and brown sugar. Sometimes a recipe may call for corn syrup, molasses, or honey. If a recipe just says *sugar*, it means granulated sugar.

About Organics

Organic foods are grown without **synthetic** fertilizers and **pesticides**. This is good for the earth. And, recent studies show that organic foods may be more nutritious than **conventionally** grown foods.

Organic foods used to be hard to find. But now you can find organic versions of most foods. Organic foods are more expensive than conventionally grown foods. Families must decide for themselves whether to spend extra for organic foods.

EGGS

Eggs come in many sizes. Use large eggs unless the recipe says otherwise. Bring eggs to room temperature before you add them to the batter.

BAKING SODA AND BAKING POWDER

Baking soda and baking powder are common **leavening** agents. Leavening agents are ingredients that make baked goods rise.

Tip

Since leavening makes quick breads rise, you'd think that adding more would make even taller loaves. But the opposite is true. Too much leavening makes such big air bubbles that they pop. Then you are left with a loaf that's as flat as a pancake!

MILK

You can use whatever milk you have, whether it is skim, low fat, or whole milk. Substituting usually won't noticeably affect the quality of what you're making.

SALT

You may be surprised to see salt in a dessert recipe. Salt is a flavor **enhancer**. It enhances the flavors in your baked goods, whether they are sweet or **savory**.

EXTRACTS

There are many flavoring **extracts** used in baking. Some of these are vanilla, almond, and maple. You will probably use vanilla extract most often. Vanilla extract is made from the beans or seedpods of tropical orchids.

NUTS

Nuts, usually walnuts or pecans, add flavor to baked goods. Luckily, you can buy them already sliced or chopped!

FRUITS AND VEGETABLES

Many quick breads feature fruits and vegetables. You can use fresh or frozen produce. If you use frozen produce, be sure to thaw it first. Sometimes recipes call for citrus zest. The zest is the colored part of the citrus fruit's skin. The oils in the skins are very flavorful, so a little zest goes a long way!

Cool Techniques

These are the techniques that bakers use. If you can't remember how to do something, just reread these pages.

MEASURING DRY INGREDIENTS

Dip the measuring spoon or measuring cup into whatever you're measuring. Use a butter knife to scrape off the excess.

MIXING DRY INGREDIENTS

Unless the recipe says otherwise, always stir the dry ingredients together first. Measure them into a bowl and stir them with a fork or a whisk.

CREAMING

Creaming means beating something until it is smooth and creamy. When baking, you often need to cream butter. Unless the recipe says otherwise, use butter that is near room temperature.

GREASING A PAN

Butter wrappers are great for greasing pans. If you don't have one, use waxed paper and a bit of butter. Run the paper and butter all around the inside of the pan. There should be a light coating of butter on the bottom and sides.

FLOURING A PAN

Sometimes you will need to flour the pan after you grease it. Sprinkle about a tablespoon of flour in the greased pan. Hold the pan with one hand over the sink. Tap its side firmly with the other hand. As you tap, twist and turn the pan to move the flour around. When all the surfaces are lightly coated, dump out the extra flour.

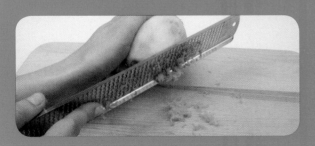

ZESTING CITRUS FRUIT

Gently scrape the fruit over the small holes of a grater or citrus zester. Just remove the colored part of the skin. Then chop the zest with a small knife. The pieces should be no longer than ¼ inch.

TESTING A LOAF OF QUICK BREAD FOR DONENESS

1. Remove the pan from the oven.

2. Stick a tester into the center of the loaf and pull it back out. You can use a knife, a wooden skewer, or a toothpick. If no gooey batter sticks to the tester, the bread is done.

3. If the bread isn't done, put it back in the oven. Check it again in a few minutes.

REMOVING A LOAF FROM A PAN

Cool the loaf according to the directions in the recipe. **Insert** a butter knife between the loaf and the side of the pan. Run it all the way around the loaf once. Turn the loaf pan upside down on top of the rack. Lightly tap the pan. Then lift it off of the loaf.

Cool Cornbread

Cornbread is great with chili or a summer salad!

MAKES ONE 8-INCH SQUARE,
ABOUT 9 PIECES

INGREDIENTS

- 1 cup stone-ground cornmeal
- 1 cup flour
- 2 teaspoons baking powder
- ½ teaspoon salt
- 2 eggs
- 1 cup milk
- ¼ cup vegetable oil
- 2 tablespoons honey

TOOLS:

8-inch square pan
mixing bowls
measuring cups

measuring spoons
whisk
wooden spoon

cooling rack
oven mitts

16

1 Preheat the oven to 425 degrees. Grease the pan.

2 Whisk together the cornmeal, flour, baking powder, and salt. Set the dry ingredients aside for now.

3 In another bowl, whisk together the eggs, milk, vegetable oil, and honey. Working quickly, stir the dry ingredients into the wet ingredients.

4 Pour the batter into the greased pan.

5 Bake for about 25 minutes. The top should be golden brown and the edges should pull away from the pan.

6 Cool on a cooling rack for about 5 minutes, then turn the pan over on the rack to remove the cornbread from the pan. Serve warm or at room temperature.

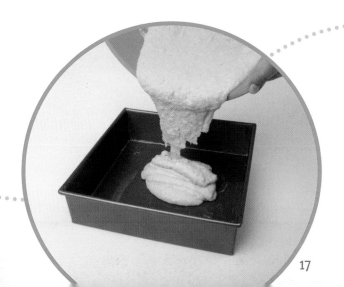

Super Cool!

> Add 1 cup of fresh or frozen corn kernels to the batter when you stir in the dry ingredients.

> Add ½ cup of grated cheddar cheese to the dry ingredients.

> Dice 1 jalapeño pepper and add it to the wet ingredients.

Bodacious Banana Bread

Banana bread is the best thing that
ever happened to overripe bananas!

MAKES 1 LOAF

INGREDIENTS

1¾ cups sifted flour

1 tablespoon
baking powder

½ teaspoon salt

⅓ cup butter

⅔ cup sugar

2 eggs

1 pound (3 to 4)
really ripe bananas

TOOLS: sifter   measuring cups   mixing bowls   mixer and beaters   oven mitts   cutting board
loaf pan   measuring spoons   whisk   cooling rack   knife

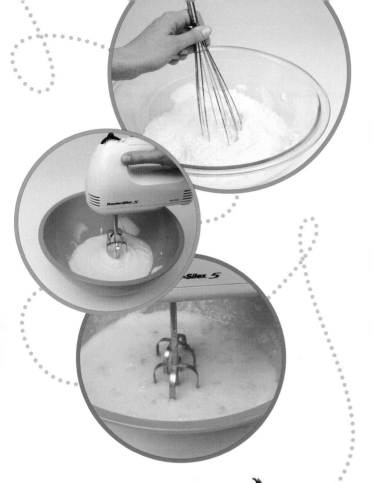

1 Preheat the oven to 350 degrees. Grease a loaf pan.

2 Whisk together the flour, baking powder, and salt in a mixing bowl.

3 In another mixing bowl, cream the butter until it is light and fluffy.

4 Add the sugar and the eggs and beat for another minute.

5 Add the peeled bananas to the egg mixture. Beat just until they are mixed in.

6 Stir in the dry ingredients. Stir just until mixed.

7 Pour the batter into the prepared loaf pan.

8 Bake for about 60 minutes. A knife **inserted** in the middle of the loaf should come out clean. Cool on a cooling rack for about 10 minutes. Then remove the loaf from the pan and let it cool completely.

Tip

Ripe bananas with black spots are perfect for making banana bread. If your bananas get ripe but you don't have time to bake, toss them in the freezer. Allow the bananas to thaw before baking with them.

Zesty Zucchini Bread

MAKES 2 LOAVES

Who knew squash could taste so good!

INGREDIENTS

- 3 cups flour
- 1 teaspoon salt
- 1 teaspoon baking soda
- ¼ teaspoon baking powder
- 3 eggs
- 1 cup vegetable oil
- 1½ cups sugar
- 2 medium zucchini, shredded with a grater (about 2 cups)
- 1 tablespoon lemon zest
- 1 tablespoon vanilla extract
- 1 tablespoon cinnamon
- ¼ teaspoon nutmeg
- 1 cup chopped walnuts (optional)

TOOLS: grater / zester / 2 loaf pans / mixing bowls / whisk / measuring cups / measuring spoons / wooden spoon / silicone spatula / cooling rack / oven mitts

1 Preheat the oven to 350 degrees. Grease and flour two loaf pans.

2 Whisk together the flour, salt, baking soda, and baking powder in a bowl. Set the bowl aside.

3 In another mixing bowl, combine the eggs, vegetable oil, sugar, zucchini, lemon zest, vanilla, cinnamon, and nutmeg. Stir just until mixed.

4 Stir in the dry ingredients. Add the walnuts, if you are using them.

5 Pour the mixture into the prepared loaf pans.

6 Bake for about 60 minutes. A toothpick **inserted** in the middle of a loaf should come out clean.

7 Cool the bread on a cooling rack for about 5 minutes. Then remove the loaves from the pans and set them on the rack. Let them cool completely.

MAKES 2 LOAVES

Country Pumpkin Bread

Try this spicy pumpkin bread toasted and topped with a smear of butter or cream cheese. Delish!

INGREDIENTS

- 2⅔ cups flour
- 2 teaspoons baking soda
- 1½ teaspoons salt
- 1 15-ounce can pumpkin (not pumpkin pie filling)
- 3 cups sugar
- 4 eggs
- 1 cup vegetable oil
- ⅔ cup water
- 2 teaspoons nutmeg
- 2 teaspoons cinnamon
- 1½ teaspoons ground cloves
- 1 teaspoon allspice
- 1 cup chopped walnuts (optional)

TOOLS:
mixing bowls
measuring cups
measuring spoons

whisk
wooden spoon
silicone spatula

2 loaf pans
cooling rack
oven mitts

1 Preheat the oven to 325 degrees.

2 Whisk together the flour, baking soda, and salt. Set the bowl aside.

3 In another mixing bowl, combine the pumpkin, sugar, eggs, vegetable oil, water, nutmeg, cinnamon, ground cloves, and allspice. Stir just until the ingredients are mixed.

4 Stir in the flour mixture. Add the walnuts, if you are using them.

5 Pour the mixture into ungreased loaf pans.

6 Bake for about 90 minutes. A toothpick **inserted** in the middle of a loaf should come out clean.

7 Cool the bread on a cooling rack for about 15 minutes. Then remove the loaves from the pans and set them on the rack. Let them cool completely.

Good Morning Muffins

MAKES ABOUT 16 MUFFINS

A tasty way to start your day!

INGREDIENTS

1¾ cups flour

½ cup bran flakes

2 teaspoons baking soda

2 teaspoons cinnamon

½ teaspoon salt

3 eggs

1¼ cups sugar

1 cup vegetable oil

1 tablespoon vanilla extract

2 cups shredded carrots (about 6 carrots)

¼ cup applesauce or 1 apple (peeled, cored, and grated)

½ cup raisins

¼ cup sweetened flaked coconut

½ cup chopped walnuts (optional)

butter (optional)

TOOLS: grater · muffin pan · mixing bowls · measuring cups · measuring spoons · whisk · wooden spoon · cooling rack · oven mitts

1 Preheat the oven to 350 degrees. Butter the cups of the muffin pan.

2 Whisk together the flour, bran flakes, baking soda, cinnamon, and salt. Set this bowl aside for now.

3 In another bowl, whisk together the eggs, sugar, vegetable oil, and vanilla. Then stir in the carrots, applesauce, raisins, and coconut. Add the walnuts, if you are using them.

4 Use a wooden spoon to stir in the dry ingredients. Stir just until the dry ingredients are mixed in.

5 Use a ⅓ cup measuring cup to fill the cups of the muffin pan. Fill each cup almost to the top.

6 Bake for 30 minutes. The muffin tops should spring back when you touch them lightly.

7 Put the muffin pan on a cooling rack for about 5 minutes. Then turn the pan over and tap the bottom until the muffins fall out. Let the muffins cool completely on the rack.

Marvelous Monkey Bread

MAKES ABOUT
15 SERVINGS

Sweet, warm monkey bread is a simply marvelous treat!

INGREDIENTS

- 3 7.5-ounce cans refrigerated biscuits
- 2 tablespoons cinnamon
- ½ cup sugar
- ½ cup pecans or walnuts
- ½ cup raisins
- 6 tablespoons butter
- ¾ cup packed brown sugar

TOOLS: tube pan or Bundt pan   measuring cups   plastic bag   silicone spatula   oven mitts
kitchen scissors   measuring spoons   small saucepan   cooling rack

1 Preheat the oven to 350 degrees. Grease a tube pan or a Bundt pan.

2 Separate the biscuits. Cut each one in half with clean kitchen scissors. Mix the cinnamon and the sugar in a medium-sized plastic bag. Put about 10 biscuit pieces in the bag. Shake the bag until they are coated. Put the coated biscuit pieces in the bottom of the pan.

3 When the bottom of the pan is covered, sprinkle on some of the raisins and nuts. Coat more biscuit pieces and arrange them in another layer. Sprinkle on more raisins and nuts. Continue layering biscuit pieces with raisins and nuts until they are all gone.

4 Put the butter and the brown sugar in a small saucepan and heat on medium high. Bring the mixture to a boil. Ask an adult helper to pour the hot mixture over the layered biscuits.

5 Bake for 35 minutes. Cool on a cooling rack for about 10 minutes.

6 Turn the pan over on a plate. Tap the bottom to loosen the monkey bread from the pan. Serve the bread while it's still warm.

Savory Herb Pull-Aparts

MAKES ABOUT 15 SERVINGS

Garlic and fresh herbs make this bread a special treat!

INGREDIENTS

- ¼ cup butter
- 1 clove garlic
- 3 7.5-ounce cans refrigerated biscuits
- 1 cup shredded Italian cheese mix (with Asiago, Parmesan, and Romano cheeses)

HERBS

- 1 tablespoon chopped fresh parsley
- 1 tablespoon chopped fresh oregano
- 1 tablespoon chopped fresh thyme

TOOLS: tube pan or Bundt Pan   garlic press   measuring cups   knife   cooling rack
small saucepan   pastry brush   measuring spoons   cutting board   oven mitts

1. Preheat the oven to 350 degrees. Grease a tube pan or a Bundt pan.

2. Melt the butter in a small saucepan over medium heat. Use a garlic press to squeeze the garlic into the warm butter.

3. Separate the biscuits. Brush a third of the biscuits with garlic butter. Cover the bottom of the pan with the buttered biscuits. Sprinkle a third of the herbs and a third of the cheese over the biscuits.

4. Butter half of the remaining biscuits and place them in the pan. Sprinkle herbs and cheese over the second layer. Brush the rest of the biscuits with garlic butter and put them in the pan. Top the biscuits with the remaining herbs and cheese.

5. Bake for about 35 minutes. The top of the bread should be golden brown. Cool on a cooling rack for about 10 minutes.

6. Turn the pan over on a plate. Tap the bottom to loosen the bread from the pan. Serve the bread while it is still warm.

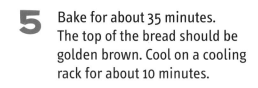

Wrap It Up!

Tips for serving, storing, and sharing the treats you make!

It's hard to beat quick bread that is still warm from the oven. But toasted banana, zucchini, or pumpkin bread comes pretty close. Just cut a slice and pop it in the toaster. Now that's yummy!

If you and your family can't eat the bread you make right away, you can freeze it. Just wrap the loaf in plastic wrap and slip it into a freezer bag. This works well for muffins too. Other breads, such as monkey bread and pull-aparts, are best eaten within a day or two of baking them.

Of course, you can always give away your baked goods too. You could wrap the cooled loaf in plastic wrap and tie a nice ribbon around it. Or, line a small basket with a pretty napkin and fill it with muffins or sliced quick bread.

Glossary

bacteria – tiny, one-celled organisms that can only be seen through a microscope.

bodacious – remarkable or extraordinary.

conventional – in the usual way.

enhance – to increase or improve.

extract – a product made by concentrating the juices taken from something such as a plant.

germ – a tiny, living organism that can make people sick.

insert – to put something into something else.

leavening – a substance such as yeast or baking soda that makes baked goods rise.

pesticide – a substance used to kill insects.

savory – tasty and flavorful but not sweet.

synthetic – produced artificially through chemistry.

Web Sites

To learn more about cool baking, visit ABDO Publishing Company on the World Wide Web at **www.abdopublishing.com.** Web sites about cool baking are featured on our Book Links page. These links are routinely monitored and updated to provide the most current information available.

Index